T0198785

Café Trinity

Serving Up a Delicious Selection of Poems
to Satisfy All of Your Senses

Poems by:

Wendy Lo

Illustrations by:

Mitsuba & Haruno Ranmaru

To order additional copies of this book, contact:
Xlibris
844-714-8691
www.Xlibris.com
Orders@Xlibris.com

ISBN:	Softcover	978-1-5992-6094-5
	Hardcover	978-1-5992-6268-0
	EBook	978-1-6641-7253-1

Print information available on the last page.

Rev. date: 04/28/2021

Acknowledgements

The author and illustrators would like to thank everyone who has given them invaluable support and inspiration: their family, friends, teachers, Abigail P. and Ernestine P. for inspiration, the lovely ladies of Toyama writing circle: Chinita A., Jo O., Lisa L., Melissa T., and Amber C. for their encouragement and advice, and Mr. Nagata and Mr. Ota for looking out for us.

✣Menu✣

Main Course:
Love

Chef's Recommendation:
Hope & Inner Strength

Side Order:
Life

Main Course
Love

And Yet We Never Met...

Everyday we cross the same paths,

take the same train, buy an apple from the same lady,

Yet we've never met...

Everyday we follow each other's previous step,

Yet we've never met...

We drank from the same fountain, saw the same

movie, and ate at the same restaurant,

But yet we never met...

10, a 100, a thousand times we could've ... but yet we've never met...

Many times in city of lights our shadows secretly greeted one another,

But never had they bothered to introduce us to each other.

Often times the only thing that separated us was a thin wall, a telephone stall,

or a wrong call...but yet we've never met...

Several times our umbrellas had intimately nestled in each other folds,

in an umbrella stand on rainy days... but yet we've never met...

We wished upon the same star and gazed fascinated at

the same blue moon, but yet we've never met...

In a crowded elevator, at either ends of a long line,

and at the other side of a platform,

But yet we've never met...

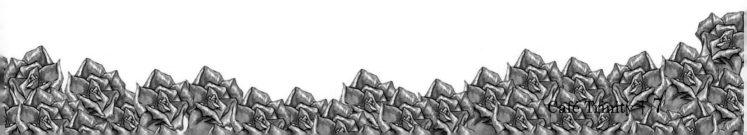

At the library we borrowed the same books one after the other,

Leafed through the same pages, uttered the same words,

The books familiar with our touch more so than we… but yet we've never met.

A blue pen you found at the station,

A blue pen I lost at the station,

A melody you hummed while waiting for the train,

A sweet melody I heard hummed somewhere in a distance,

But yet we've never met…

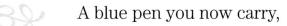 A blue pen you now carry,

A sweet melody I now hum,

And yet we've never met…

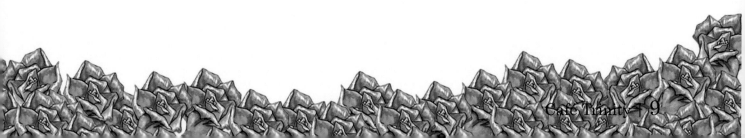

Awake in our beds, imagining each other,

A faceless figure, with no name and place,

All an empty answer to a curious question… because we've never met.

Our existence of one another only known by the observers

of this tragic story,

How many more encounters will we have

and still have never met?

We could be each other's soul mate,

And by the time we know it may be too late,

Is that the cruel hand dealt by lady fate?

At the moment there is no sadness or regret,

for we have never met….

A Dinner Among the Flowers

A soft yet vibrant appearance of a blush,

A kiss from the cupid that secretly sits upon your shoulder,

A smile sneaks from your lips and runs away to me,

It whispers your secret to my heart,

A word of love not spoken… yet understood,

Two hands entwined to confess what not was said,

Spring heeds not the cold of winter,
Yet she blooms against the rules of nature,
Taking with her the inhibitions of the frigid cold,
As we savor the taste of each other,
"While enjoying a dinner among the flowers."

Autumn's Confession

The autumn leaves have turned,

Falling into winter's shade,

Covered in the leaves we held each other as if this was the last day,

Blessed by the warm caress of the sun's ray,

A change in the seasons as well as in the heart,

A new beginning for our love to start,

A secret that was held in solitude,

Has been brought forth with determined fortitude,

A confession witnessed by autumn's colors,

That you are for me, and no other.

Luminance

Illuminate my heart, and cast away the shadows of my past,

Illuminate the night sky with your ethereal brilliance,

Illuminate the room with your charisma,

Illuminate the halls of all the heroes of the past with
your gallantry and valor,

Illuminate my soul, and fill me with your radiance,

Illuminate the world with your magnificent presence.

Chef's Recommendations
Hope
&
Inner Strength

What Has Not Been...

I've been drifting along all this time,
Searching, trying to find,
Something that has not been,
Bound to the pursuit of something that can't be seen,
Enchained by this yearning for it to magically appear,
But the wait has extended past my youthful years,
Contemplating if I missed the chance,
But was too blind by the hunt that I passed it without a thoughtful glance,
Anxious emotions stir in my heart,
Locked up too long since the start,
Longing to see the beautiful strokes of a romantic's art,
To hear the rhapsody of a joyful heart,

I never played by the rules of society,
By my own rules I fatally built up an impenetrable wall,
So tall and discouraging to the few that have braved the challenge,
But yet no one has ever surpassed it and met their fall,
A fortress of daydreams that fogs ones mind,
That leads me to my crime,
An obsession to stalk the desire of meeting this great treasure,
Every thought and action enraptured,
By the thought of an ecstatic sensation that would fill me by the discovery,
Euphoric hope that what I long for is longing for me in mutual reverie,
How far will this worn traveler have to travel?
To find the one thing that can make her
bounded heart unravel.

Living Today for Tomorrow

The moon has risen all the world seems calm,

The night has fallen, to the one I love,

May the whispers of my heart reach you way above heaven's door,

Carried to you by the wings of the dove.

The countless, hours, days, and years have come and gone,

Leaving me alone along the path,

Longing to see you as my youth has come to pass,

Vividly I imagine you… still sitting there beside me,

The memories of you will never go vague in my mind… at any time.

Far off in the distance I hear a sigh,

Could you be nearby? And not have died?

As I cry, I see your mischievous smile,

The bright laughter, and your every day patterns,

Your random acts, and habitual tact,

Your joy for life and all the strife,

Always cherishing the moments that has passed and yet to be,

Always marching forward to see,

So much is waiting to be done, and new dreams to come,

I realized our time has passed, but my memory of you will last.

Although frightened that I am, I will firmly stand,

And by your memories and all that you cherish I will carry on,

To see each and every day that dawns.

Metamorphosis

Morphing, changing…

Once small, miniscule… unsightly,

Hiding, scared… quiet solitude in one's own protective cocoon,

The real me hidden… shrouded under layers of self-doubt,

Pushing, crying, whispering, listening, screaming…

in this sound-proof gawky shell,

Growing, hoping, learning… enlightened.

Morphing, changing…

Petals of Self-doubt peeling, withering, falling…

Colors, brilliance, light, blooming…. Opened.

Metamorphosed…

Is this the real me?

Caged Bird

Mother was born within enclosed compounds of tradition,
Behind the bars to sing and perform her maidenly duties,
A sheltered life and a sheltered mind,
A caged bird…
Hatched in a different time and place,
Your plumage and songs unique, carries it own careful grace,
Your mind has wandered and saw past the iron grate,
To fly higher and farther from the confines of an oppressive past,
To taste the winds and the colors of the vastness that awaits,
A caged bird no more at last.

This is me

My ideas are too big to be confined,

My opinions too loud to silence,

My attitude is graceful and rough,

My style speaks of originality,

My experiences comprehensible only to me,

My emotions a raging tempest and a calm morning breeze,

My dreams far too high to reach, yet enough to graze the tip,

My hope keeps me reaching,

My fantasies take me to places unexplored,

My opportunities lost and taken,

My self I love and hate,

My imperfections I have accepted,

My perfections I believe I have,

My inner strength makes me a survivor,

My heart reserved for special treasures,

My soul displayed for those who can see,

My mind free to roam unquestioned,

My life my own to free...

Parfum de Memoire

Your words dance into my ears,
Lost aloft the crowd,
A whirlwind of memories lift me,
I spend the nights awake wondering if you are thinking about me too,
My thoughts of you ride off into the pale moonlit night,

The piano is playing your story, as the fragrance of your past drifts through the notes,
Its alluring scent captivates me again,
The reminiscence of your kiss stills lingers on my lips,
The melody resonates the sadness in my heart,
In this eerie silence that cuts through the crowded room,

I turn and catch an apparition of you smiling back,
I part my lips to speak, but you turn and disappeared before I could say…
I loved you.

Regrets and promises remembered and lost,
A lullaby of our blissful moments,
Once was there, has now been buried deep,
A candle at the end of its wick, struggling to burn,
A feeling rekindled by your essence,
That dances beautifully in my mind,

Again I sit here, expecting for you to walk through the door,
Again another night lost…moored, by the desire to see you once more,
A seat, vacant, waiting for its owner to return,
Escaping the flow of time, your beauty ingrained in the mind,
While mine is fading with time.

Side Order
Life

One of the Forgotten...

A white ghost sleepily creeps out of open lips,
A breath of life that decides to journey,
Vanishing into the night air to join the others,
A sudden cold embrace that breaks the warmth once held,
Frigid stares and pitied looks unnoticed by you,
One of the forgotten...

Laughter and voices heard from a distance...
growing audibly loud...pass you... then fade quickly to nothing...
like a car speeding by,
Too busy to stop and give you a ride,
A cruel repetition of a broken record,
One of the forgotten...

The warmth of hope that once shined within has grown dim,
Casting long shadows,
A soundless cry unheard,
Muffled by the silent answer given,
One of the forgotten...

Children

Sometimes children are sweet adorable little angels,
Sometimes they are mean little brats,
Sometimes they could be brutally honest,
Sometimes they'll lie without a flinch,
Sometimes they are brave and daring,
Sometimes they are shy and afraid,
Sometimes they want to try everything and anything,
Sometimes they are more finicky than a cat.
Sometimes they are obedient,
Sometimes they are rebellious,
Sometimes they make you want to hug them,
Sometimes they make you scream,
Sometimes they are clever,
Sometimes they are naïve,
Sometimes they are innocent,
Sometimes they are guilty,
Sometimes they make you laugh,
Sometimes they make you cry,
Sometimes they make you proud,
Sometimes they disappoint you,
Sometimes they are respectful,
Sometimes they don't care who you are,
Sometimes they care about others,
Sometimes they bully them,
Sometimes they'll help you,
Sometimes they'll ignore you,
Sometimes they give you comfort,
Sometimes they give you problems,
Sometimes they are responsible,
Sometimes they are reckless,

Sometimes they are popular,
Sometimes they are unnoticed,
Sometimes they are sociable,
Sometimes they are alone,
Sometimes they try their best,
Sometimes they give up,
Sometimes they are fair,
Sometimes they cheat,
Sometimes they heal you,
Sometimes they hurt you,
Sometimes they are interested,
Sometimes they are bored,
Sometimes they surprise you,
Sometimes they horrify you,
Sometimes they are carefree,
Sometimes they are demanding,
Sometimes they love you,
Sometimes they hate you,
Children…
Don't they remind you of adults?

Humanity's Fault

Flowers blow in the wind,

As we bury our kin,

Lives lost,

But at what cost?

Boys not yet men,

Away they are sent,

Heroes are born and enemies are sworn,

So dark and cold,

The heaviness in our souls,

Both sides determined to be right,

As children huddle together in fright,

Fires ablaze, sending confusion and

anger throughout the endless days.

In the night a prayer is spoken,

To those who will never be woken,

A hopeful prayer shared by many,

That there was no such word as "enemy."

A sorrowful song is heard among the bombs,

The endless cries, as loved ones die,

An infinite flow of battles throughout human history,

or different reasons, always bringing change and misery,

Can we ever reconcile our differences,

to exist side by side with no grievances?

The Eternal Game

A cold finger that runs down your spine
and brings a frigid chill in the air,
A shadow that haunts our every move… at every moment,
Patiently waiting, diligently watching the sands of our time
slowly trickle till the end.
At the descent of the last grain, the dark harbinger calls,
With sharp swiftness all is taken…
The last grain resting at the peak of the mountain,
As if overturning the verdict, a hand reaches out,
The sands of time once more are falling,
The last grain… now the first… a new life born…
And so begins again the little game
that Life and Death plays.

The Modern Geisha

A glittered lip parts to speak,

A butterfly eye winks,

Two golden suns shimmering upon the cheeks,

Fireworks of damaged hair bursting forth,

A strange animal awkwardly waddling,

On flashy sharp stilettos,

Bearing the pain for their fashionable egos,

A modern geisha.

Tsunami

An uncontrollable beast raging forth,

Engulfed by its awesome presence,

Lost in an instance…

Lifted, swept, carried, and swallowed,

Others…eaten alive, swallowed whole,

Whirled around in its mouth, as if savoring

the taste of its delicate morsel.

Swirling, grasping, searching, fearing, fighting the descent

into the monster's bottomless stomach,

Reaching, pulling, pushing, thrown about in its bowels,

Instinctive struggle to defeat the hold of the beast.

Burning inside, reaching, kicking, writhing to be free…

For the light, the heavenly air above,

Wrestling, climbing, bursting through to the top,

A moment of release from the painful clutches of the beast,

To see Apollo smiling gaily, as if unaware of Poseidon's wrath below,

Once again eaten, by the relentless beast,

Strength lost, and the luster of life… succumbed to the icy hold

of the watery catacombs of Poseidon,

Another voice lost in the eternal symphony of the waves.

Café Trinity

Serving Up a Delicious Selection of Poems
to Satisfy All of Your Senses

Printed in the United States
by Baker & Taylor Publisher Services